Armando and Maisie

Armando and Maisie

Poems by

John Maynard

© 2025 John Maynard. All rights reserved.
This material may not be reproduced in any form, published,
reprinted, recorded, performed, broadcast,
rewritten, or redistributed without
the explicit permission of John Maynard.
All such actions are strictly prohibited by law.

Cover design by Shay Culligan
Cover image by John Maynard

ISBN: 978-1-63980-790-1
Library of Congress Control Number: 2025939431

Kelsay Books
502 South 1040 East, A-119
American Fork, Utah 84003
Kelsaybooks.com

Contents

Introduction: *My* Armando	11
Past, Present, and Future, or, a Dog's Life	12
Armando	13
Armando Considers Shaving	14
Armando Not There	15
Armando and Maisie	17
Armando Accepts	18
Armando Makes a Life	19
Armando's Popularity	20
Armando Makes Pictures	21
Spirit Food	22
Armando Absent	23
Armando on Marriage	24
Armando Pleases Maisie	25
Emotional Physics	26
Practical Aesthetics	27
Twenty Dollar Bill for Armando	28
Armando, Loving All Dogs, Still Discriminates	29
Armando's New Shirt	30
I Am Armando	31
Raccoon Story	32
Armando and the Gentry	34
Armando Leaves Early; Maisie Defies the Laws of Physics	35
Armando's New Hat and Coat	36
Armando Sights a Hawk	37
I Give Armando a Twenty Dollar Bill Again	38
We Just Miss Armando	39
Armando's Sleeping Bag	40
Armando on Change	41
Armando on the Defensive	42
Armando in Distress	43
Armando Paints with Peanut Butter	44
Armando Takes Space, Leaves Time	45

Maisie Makes Armando a Little Jealous	47
Maisie Meets Armando Unexpectedly	48
Armando Explains Squirrels' Morning Timing	49
Armando's Dark Side, Very Dark	50
Treats from Armando	51
Maisie Meets Armando After Sicknesses of Both	52
We Fail to Meet Armando on a Day When Rain Is Expected, with Simple and Complicated Responses	53
Armando Offers Comfort	54
Armando Still Wants Maisie's Coat	55
Armando's Den in the Park Is Discovered (by No Person)	56
Maisie Visits Armando *in extremis* and We Talk Little	57
Armando Happens on Maisie Doing Poorly, Maybe Says Goodbye	58
Tale's End	60

Introduction: *My* Armando

Everyone who knows him—
And many people do
Who come through the park woods
And exchange a friendly word
With his welcome face—
Everyone has his own Armando
And all of them true for them—
And true perhaps for Armando
Too, who is a man of plain face
And many sides. This is *my*
Armando. I hope it pleases you
And pleases him if he sees it.
I didn't make it up
But I made it nonetheless.

Past, Present, and Future, or, a Dog's Life

I meet a man in the park
In a quiet woody part.
He says: life lives itself
In three parts: future,
Past, and present. I am saying
Live in the present. This moment
Is, this is what there is.
Dogs—looks at my dog—know this.
Present is all we have.
He wants to say, seize
The moment: doesn't have the words.
He speaks, his speech is gone.
I intend to remember
What he says. I write:
The moment's gone, the dog's
Moved on. He said dogs were
Happy in the moment.
My dog was miserable yesterday.
Today she's happy, as happy
As she was miserable.
I tried to say to him
So dogs suffer more.
He didn't hear
And does not understand.

Armando

On a lovely day in June
I met the man in the woods again
And we shot the breeze
For a while. We'd passed
Some other times and I knew
His face, a genial man
Friendly and philosophical
In a normal human way—
About life, time, the comic
Ways of people and of animals.
He liked to feed the squirrels.
Once before I'd asked his name
So I dared to say Alfonso,
Good talking to you, as I
Went along. Armando's the name
He said and laughed, easily.

Armando Considers Shaving

Armando said he went to Coney Island,
Had a swim: it was cool and nice
And he thought of shaving off his beard.
I said, don't do that. I won't know you.
He said, and I won't know myself
But that's not so bad. And he thought
Why not shave my head while I'm at it?
I said, you have some hair on your head—
Not bare. Shave it off you'll get lots
Of sun. He said, he always had it shaved
But he had a bet once with an Indian guy
Who ran a deli. He'd get free coffee for a week
If he had more hair than the deli man.
He grew it and got lots of coffee, but here
Who needs it? What advantage does it serve?
How will I ever know you then? I said.
Remember, he said, I'm the man with the painted box.
No, I said, I know it will be another man with
A painted box, but at least I'll know the box.

Armando Not There

Maisie the dog
Was looking for Armando:
The man
Who always sat in the woods
Feeding the squirrels
And would give her
A warm embrace
And she an even warmer
Return, shaking both tail and body.
But he wasn't there
Today.
She went right up to the bench
Where he always sat
With his funny little box.
She sniffed about and realized
That's where he should have been.
And she looked sad
And left.
Perhaps another day, I said.
I thought, if Armando was dead
Someone should have put a plaque
On one of those benches:
Armando sat here, Maisie looked for him
Every day and so did many another dog
And now he's not here:
To feed the squirrels
And to dispense each day
Happy wisdom.
He was there the next day
And they embraced

He saying as always
He wished he had her beautiful warm coat.
That made her happy.
And him too
Every day that they met.

Armando and Maisie

Maisie loves Armando
Who feeds the birds in the woods
All winter long in a great gray coat
With the spirit of a Santa Claus
Come up from South America
Somewhere. And he loves her.
He says, give me that white coat
Of yours, let me have that one.
She says, take it off
If you like. I give it to you
Because you are my best friend
In all the world. He says
Thank you, Maisie, but I know you need it
To sit in the snow and chew your stick.
And I'll feed the birds again today.
Sure to say, come next meeting
He'll be out doing the same happy bird feed
And they'll have the same discussion.
That's what friendship is, the same discussion.

Armando Accepts

At his ease
Reclining on a park bench
Deep in the woods
Where it was cool
And the breezes were gentle
Armando said:
The past is history
The future is a mystery
The present is a gift—
Which I take.
His acceptance was unqualified.
He thought neither of the joyous effusions of spring
He'd left behind or winter coming on
With its cold shocks and circumambient ice.

Armando Makes a Life

He makes his heaven
In spite of all, in spite of
Hell. In spite of the way
They treat men down at the shelter
(Where he wills never to go).
With his box of paints and pens,
His drawing pad, little treats
For the squirrels that he picks up
Here and there, he forswears the shelter
And makes a life, happy,
In the woods, not a care.
Not a fear and wishes all
Good morrow, whoever they happen
To be: habituals, strangers,
They from other countries
As he was himself.
Happy to spend the day
Whispering to every dog
Who comes by, keeping
The squirrels in feed.
So proud watching one day
Where a coyote moved into the park
Beneath a big rock.
They caught that coyote
Took it out, and took
It away. And he grieved,
Quiet by himself, for many days
And maybe thought, at least
They haven't taken *me* away.
People come over from Strawberry Fields
Just to say hello Armando,
And his courtesy is unfailing.

Armando's Popularity

I write poems about Armando
Not because he has a good
Attitude, but because he has
The right attitude. They call him
The dog whisperer, but he's also
A people whisperer and what
He says is, seize the day, enjoy life
As it comes, don't count on tomorrow,
Put off today what you can.
And he has quite a following:
Dogs, and ladies with dogs, guys
With dogs and guys on their own
Who come to see what he's up to.
And squirrels, who love his peanuts
But certainly take his philosophy
Along with the nuts. He's sitting
There even now, on his throne
In the Ramble, holding court,
Giving a seminar on taking life
As it comes and when it comes.

Armando Makes Pictures

Armando finds a stick
Or weathered board
Now and then,
Puts white backing on it,
Begins to paint.
For a strong man
Very careful, very delicate.
What's the point?
I asked him once.
He said, well I make a little money:
People sometimes buy these
When I'm done,
Sometimes I paint their dogs.
But I like to take
My pictures of the animals
In the woods—
Squirrels that come by, birds.
Today he was doing
A red cardinal
From a book.
That's cheating, I said.
He said, no,
I see many cardinals here—
Just needed to check out
The feathers and get them right.
Bright pretty moments
When he finishes them up.
We left him with his glasses on—
Deep in his work.

Spirit Food

Maisie saw Armando
And ran to him.
He saw her
And ran to her.
They care a lot about each other.
And he embraced her,
Rubbing her neck, and back,
And remarking on her beautiful coat,
As always.
Had had some trouble
With her neck:
Held it a little funny
And he rubbed and fluffed,
Rubbed and fluffed.
And he said
That's a spiritual massage
Like food for the spirit,
Combines the material and the soul's stuff.
He went along.
We went along.
That dog felt better.
That entire dog.

Armando Absent

I could see him
As we came up the hill
Sitting on a bench
Feeding the birds
With his funny little box
Of bird food and peanuts
For the squirrels.
I'm sure he was there.
But my eye fooled me.
He didn't come today:
The weather was too cold
Or something bad
Happened to him.
The dog was sure.
She ran up to
The him that wasn't
There. I told her
Armando didn't come
Today. She looked
Perplexed, sniffed
Around where he
Always came. What's
Not there our eye
(Or nose) provides,
Our heart knows
How to find.
Armando didn't come today.

Armando on Marriage

Armando says there's a park bench
Near where he does his work, painting
His pictures of dogs on driftwood,
And the plaque on it says Marry Me.
And all the couples come by
And the women stop and say
Look at that, how nice, Marry Me.
Armando shrugs his shoulders
The way their guys do who then say,
Come on, let's get moving here;
We got a long way to go.
Armando says that young people
All want to go into marriage
And the old ones all want to come out.
I said, I know what you mean:
I've had three wives. And he looked
At Maisie, and I said, three dogs too—
Then added quickly, because the first
And second died. He was okay with that.
I wasn't sure if he had ever married
And didn't think I should intrude by asking.

Armando Pleases Maisie

Armando loves the big dog Maisie,
Puts his hands with fingers outstretched
Through her long thick white fur,
Warms his hands and pleases her
A lot every day they meet.
It's a ritual and he mutters over her:
Is that coat ready, will you have that coat
For me when it turns really cold?
And Maisie jumps up, as if to say,
Help yourself Armando, I am yours completely.
Comes the spring, he tries to cool her off,
Stroking the fur up to let the air in.
He says, get it ready for next winter.
I'll be needing it. And their friendship
Goes on once or twice a week like that.
All the dogs love Armando, but Maisie
Thinks she's the favorite because
He'll get up when he sees her,
Jump a fence, go into the woods, and leave
The other dogs somewhat in the lurch.
That's the way he shows his preference
For the big dog with the long thick white hair.
And she runs between his legs
And settles down with her rear end on his foot
And looks happy. She's found him again.

Emotional Physics

Two objects cannot occupy
The same space at the same time.
She knows that. She tried
To put her bone on top of the ball.
It fell off. The other one
Is harder. An object
Cannot be in one place
And also in another place
At the same time. But
Armando should be here
In his usual place.
But we just saw him
On the road going out.
Why isn't he here?
He should be here.

Practical Aesthetics

Armando uses acrylic.
It's the only paint for him,
He says. You can let it dry,
Paint over your mistakes,
Cut your losses, and make
A perfect job. They are
Little dogs and little birds
On white background. I said,
Acrylic's so sharp and clear,
Fits your way of painting
With its bright, solid colors.
He nodded: maybe yes,
I wasn't sure. It works well, he said,
In the woods here, where some rain,
A drop of bird, could make a mess
With oils or watercolor. They're nice,
I said, and we walked away.
There was a light blue sky,
Darker water, also bright,
And a cardinal flashing red—
Sallow yellow eyes and a black spot
Between. Fall woods a happy solid orange.

Twenty Dollar Bill for Armando

I gave Armando
A twenty dollar bill.
It wasn't a sudden impulse.
I'd thought about it—
Would he be insulted?
Independence, living in the park
Was sure his goal.
But I gave it to him
Saying, must cost
Quite a lot
To get all those peanuts
And birdseed.
He said, thank you,
Yes, it does.
I hoped he'd buy
Himself something to eat
As well, though
He never seems to lack
For food.
If he's on the welfare rolls,
He's not coming off anytime soon.
And whatever age he is,
He's definitely retired.
No one ever says,
Go get a job.
And he never asks for anything.
I gave a contribution
To the chickadees and squirrels fund.
He received it with dignity.
I shouldn't have worried.
We worked it out.

Armando, Loving All Dogs, Still Discriminates

All the dogs love Armando
And to his credit he loves
All the dogs: big ones, small
Ones, fat ones, skinny ones,
Lap dogs, sheep dogs, huskies . . .
All types of dogs pass by
And give him a fond greeting.
And he greets them with equal
Fondness. Yappy dogs, silent dogs,
Every type of dog. Maybe that's why
They like him so well: because
They know he likes all kinds of dogs
And they can be whatever dog
They want to be with him.
Still Maisie says he likes her
Best of all. And that may be
The case. Why not? Her step
Is all the lighter, her eyes
That much brighter, her affection stronger.

Armando's New Shirt

Armando always dresses well
But this was fabulous.
I came around a corner
In the woods.
He was talking to two women
With a dog and he had
A big yellow shirt
Covering his whole body:
Perfect
For the first cool day of fall.
And it said across the front
In delicate lettering,
Lacoste, with a crocodile.
What a lovely shirt, I said.
He smiled, and petted Maisie
As he always does, then shyly:
I got it at Macy's.
I thought he said Maisie's
Because he always says
He'll take her coat for the winter.
No, he said, Macy's the store.
That's what I call it.
It's really M for midnight run.
They have lovely clothes
For homeless people
And sandwiches too. I told him
Lacoste was a fancy brand.
He said, of course:
It comes from Macy's
And I am a friend of Maisie's.

I Am Armando

The whole week we came by his seat
But Armando wasn't there.
Someone said he'd had a foot problem
And had to go and get it fixed.
Someone else said it was a bad time
For him. He didn't come into the woods
These days. Maisie sniffed around, knew
His smell but knew he was not there.
The birds and squirrels were cleaning up
What was left from the week before
And also wondered where he was and how
They'd do without him. Finally, one day
Maisie chose to sit just where he always
Sat. I said okay, we'll sit here and see
If he arrives. And he didn't.
And we watched the birds and the squirrels
And knew why he loved the quiet here
And saw a cardinal settle for a while.
Brilliant red. A few people came by, asked
What it was. The peace, in the heart of the city,
Was overwhelming—almost severe but lovely.
And we stayed. I said to Maisie, let's go along
But we stayed and she made no move to go.
And then it occurred to me, now I'm here
I am Armando. I am he. And peace
Settled thickly all around. Maybe he'll come
Some day and let me go my way.

Raccoon Story

There was a raccoon
Stuck in the side
Of a roof it was trying
To climb.
Michelle and Ed saw it—
And some other woman
Who was out there
Walking with them.
And they made a good
Fuss and they found
A park ranger. He had
To be careful
But he had a metal thing
Like a cage
And he got that raccoon
To drop in the cage.
The raccoon was pretty much
Dead, having his head stuck
In the side of the roof.
They said he was rather
Excited—who wouldn't be?
They took that raccoon
To rehab
To bring it back
To its life
And as far as everyone knows
The raccoon's doing okay.
And so there was generally
Celebration
And a sense
Of something accomplished.
And I, I had nothing

To do with all this,
Coming late to the story
As I did.
But I ran into Armando
And asked if he knew
The news about the raccoon
But he said he didn't.
So I got to tell it,
Make it mine.
So in a way I was
Part of the big news of the day.
And Armando even thanked me
And I said, but I still
Thank *you* for the coyote story
Not so very long ago
And how he had a den
Down in the glen nearby
And slipped out at night
To find what he could
To survive. The rangers,
Not always so perfect
As they appeared in the raccoon
Story today, had caught him
And taken him away
And it's thought
That he had his last day.

Armando and the Gentry

He's like the hermit in the play,
And genteel tourists stop
To pass a few minutes, listen
To his philosophy of life,
Which is a good one,
And move on. Oh let's
Go see Armando, they say. Off
They go, maybe taking him
A cider or coffee from the café.
He's open to all discussion
And what a pleasure to talk
With him! Everyone knows Armando.
Everyone enjoys his conversation.
Someone says, couldn't the homeless
Learn so much from him about how
To get by and someone agrees
And someone disagrees. But he's
Not homeless. Anywhere he is
He makes his home and finds comfort.

Armando Leaves Early; Maisie Defies the Laws of Physics

She ran into Armando
Just five minutes ago.
It was wet today
And he was leaving early.
But when she got
To his seat in the woods
She went crazy, running
Up to meet him, knowing
He had to be there
Because that was his seat.
No two objects, I said,
Can be in the same place
At the same time. Or,
As here, no one object can be
In two places at one time.
She looked at me like I
Was nuts. What's that
Got to do with it.
It's Armando.

Armando's New Hat and Coat

Armando bought himself
A red cap. Heavy leather
Tipping down over his eyes
In a rakish way.
Nice looking. And
I said to him
Nice looking red hat.
He said, thank you,
I'm glad you noticed.
And we talked about it.
I went away for quite a while
And when I returned
I ran into Armando
On a rainy day, leaving the park
With his wooden cart
As always. Maisie jumped him
And they had great greeting.
Then I saw an amazing thing:
He had a big red coat
Just the color of his hat.
And I said you don't have
To worry anymore about hunters
In the park, and we laughed.
He was always unmistakable.
Now he's red and unmistakable.

Armando Sights a Hawk

Armando told me
As he was leaving.
It was a big hawk
Up in a tree
With a red tail
And I found it
Up in that tree
Sitting as quiet
As Armando does
When he just studies
The scene. First I thought
It was a bird's nest
But it had a head
And the head moved about.
A little squirrel came almost
Up to it. And a man came by.
I showed him the hawk.
He said Armando had showed it
To him. And we both said
It's a pretty brave squirrel
To go right up to
A hawk. But nothing happened.
He went his way
And I went the other.
The hawk stayed
Staring at it all.
I'll have to mention
That I did see him
Next time I see Armando.

I Give Armando a Twenty Dollar Bill Again

I give Armando
A twenty dollar bill again
And tell him
It's for the Birdseed Fund
And he laughs and thanks me.
He says, for the birds.
But I guess he'll share it
Fifty-fifty.
And I think, big deal—
Hardly last a day or two,
Keep hunger off.
And another side of me thinks
Fat man he is.
He's healthy enough
And he could get a job.
And I think, what job
Could he get?
What he does
Is the right job for him.
I think, I'll give him another twenty
Another day. For work done
Keeping the birds and himself alive.
Also, for wisdom in the woods
And unfailing good humor—
Which is a hard job.

Two years later:
Am I giving him enough?
Now he gives really good
Treats to Maisie and other
Dogs on top of all the birds
And squirrels: not much left
At all for himself.

We Just Miss Armando

Maisie and I came out of the path.
She sniffed and I saw Armando
Going in the other direction quite a long way away—
And moving pretty fast with his little box
Beside him—little painting box on wheels.
And Maisie saw him. And now he was
A long way away. And I decided
It was too far. And he looked hurried—
Not his better self that he got together
For the birds, the squirrels, the friends
Who dropped in to chat. An old man
With a funny box, rather tired. If
We'd run after him, would he have lit up
And had a better day? We met the squirrels
He fed that morning and the little birds.
They seemed to have had a good day already.
Maisie sniffed his bench and wanted him a lot.

Armando's Sleeping Bag

A friend gave Armando a sleeping bag.
Would, I kept asking him, it
Work down to twenty degrees minus?
And he didn't say no. I think
It was likely. Maisie was sniffing it.
He said he put a coat over it
To keep it warm and to keep it
Dry during the day. I said, I guess
You have no coldness here with that.
Not at all. What I don't like
Is people invite me in their houses.
No good air. I get sick right away.
Sleeping bag is just right for me.
And then he added, I get inside
A contractor's plastic bag before I get inside
The sleeping bag. I said, I bet
You get hot as hell. Yes, indeed.
I even begin to sweat. Then Maisie
Said it was time to go. But that was
Important: that he had a way to sleep
In the park in any weather.

Armando on Change

Hadn't seen Armando
For a couple of months.
Then ran into him
On his usual woods bench.
He said, you were away.
I said, yes. He said,
They changed that place
Where you have breakfast.
I said, oh yeah? He said,
Yeah, no more muffins
For Maisie. He said it
Sympathetically. She's going
To miss them. I said,
I guess she will.
It's one of her favorite things
Other than meeting you.
And the two of them embraced
For a while. Then I said,
That's *quite* a change.
Things change, he said.
There's always change,
Change and more change.
We looked at each other.
You're right, I said.
Maisie and I went off
Hoping for a substitute
For muffins. Things change.
There is change. Change,
Only, is always.

Armando on the Defensive

Today Armando wore
A camel beret,
Keeping the rain off
A bit, and had to defend
Himself. Some people said
He gave too much food
To animals and should cut
It back—the birds, squirrels, even
The passing dogs! What was
The point of it all, and he
With no money to speak of
And the birds and the dogs
As fat as could be.
He said, they're turning people
Against me, people I don't
Even know stop and shake
A finger: why are you being
So generous with the animals?
What's the point of it all?
He said, I don't know what
To say. But the animals, they
Aren't complaining. Armando's
Not changing his bad ways.

Armando in Distress

Once or twice
Armando found his philosophy
Growing thin, here and there
And about the edges.
Philosophy. Not religion,
Not that old dead god
Had done him no good
When his life was a hell,
Which was often the case
Large or small. Homeless shelters,
Poor charity, jobs now and then.
He found it helped to say
Grab the day,
Don't let the sun go by
Without some sunshine falling
On your face.
But now and then
It all seemed not to help.
Through the veil of philosophy
Life was exposed for what it was.
And he grieved.
But grieved alone.
Officially, that is
To all his friends
Who liked him for his approach
To sunshine and to life,
He kept the faith of his philosophy,
Buoyed up others
While he felt he had begun
To sink.

Armando Paints with Peanut Butter

We caught Armando
Over the fence in a little wood
Big jar in his hand and a little
Plastic spoon. He was painting
Peanut butter clutches in the trees.
I didn't need to ask him
What he was doing: The birds
Love it up in the trees.
Much better than having them
Come to me. And I looked
And saw all the trees had
Little webs of peanut butter
Here and there. And, yes,
The birds were busy at work
Flitting here and there, liking
It a lot. How did you know,
I asked him. What I know
I know. I don't think about it.
I know it. I said, you
And the birds too. He laughed
And went back to trimming
The trees with peanut butter.

Armando Takes Space, Leaves Time

Armando says
Our bodies are mainly space.
I thought they were mainly water.
But he's right. Any physicist
Would confirm: our bodies
Are mainly space. And,
He adds, the world is space.
And the main thing
Why we're here
Is to connect our space
With the space of the whole,
The entire universe—
To be part of that space
And that space to be in us
And part of us.
It all made sense to me
And I told him so.
But he needed no confirmation.
He was sure it was true:
Animals, he said—
Looking at Maisie—
They know this.
They connect everything,
Don't miss anything.
And I said, you're right.
And he smiled. He knew he was.
But I'd been reading
The Time Machine and so I said,
And everything is time too.
We exist as time.
We are always a moment.
He is never annoyed

But if he could have been annoyed
That was annoying.
I was sorry I said it.
He's been tired lately,
Spending less time in the woods,
Leaving earlier with his box.
Yes it takes time to connect to everything.
But in a world of spacetime,
He'd take space
And leave time back on the shelf
Of the universe.

Maisie Makes Armando a Little Jealous

Maisie met Armando
Talking with Billy
Her other friend
And she knew not
What to do.
She ran to one
Then ran to the other.
Billy was a new friend.
Armando gave her a nice belly rub
Like he always did.
She jumped up
And went to Billy.
Armando noted that.
A little later, we ran into him
With his little box walking
On a different pathway
And Maisie greeted him—
Not quite so warmly as before.
And he noted that.
I said, sorry,
You're taking off
Just as we're coming out
And he looked and smiled
And said, she'll have her friends
At the boathouse.
And I said, yes,
Our Billyboy.
And he said, yes
Our Billyboy.
We laughed.

Maisie Meets Armando Unexpectedly

Maisie was minding her business
On the sidewalk by the street
When suddenly Armando was there.
She couldn't believe it.
She sniffed his cart.
It was definitely Armando.
She jumped all over him for three minutes.
She mobbed him, rolling on the pavement
Sticking her white barrel stomach up
And wiggling her paws in the air.
She hadn't seen him for weeks
So that was special.
But that wasn't what it was all about:
We all three enjoyed the simple pleasure—
What a surprise meeting here in the street!
And she rolled at my feet
To say, look we found him here,
Out of the park, *him*—and with his cart!

Armando Explains Squirrels' Morning Timing

One day Armando was feeding his squirrels
And birds. And Maisie said, give me
Some of that, give me some of that.
And he did. But she didn't like it.
She took it in and spat it out.
And we laughed. Not too long
After that Armando said he had something
For her. It was a dog treat. And she liked it
A lot. Now every time they meet she's crazy
To see Armando (as always) and crazy
For his treat. One day she was eating
Her treat and a squirrel came by and demanded
His treat too. Armando pulled out a clutch
Of peanuts and threw it out to him.
And he sat up, perky and gay, eating his peanuts
Like men at a bar. I said, if I let
Maisie go she would be after that squirrel
In a second. And Armando said, clutching
His cap for emphasis, those squirrels
Are smart. Before nine o'clock you never
See them. After that, they're all out,
All the time, every day. I was puzzled:
Why nine o'clock? Is that when you get up
And start to feed them? No, I'm up way
Before then. He looked kindly on my ignorance.
It's because the dogs are not allowed
Off leash after nine. The squirrels come down,
They know it's safe, and they run around
Happily. That seemed the truth to me
So I left it at that and we went our way.

Armando's Dark Side, Very Dark

Billy says, and probably Billy knows,
Armando once had a dark side, drugs, gangs,
Anger, violence, a temper out of control.

He keeps an even keel every day,
Looks for the best from the world,
And tries to find the best within.
And Maisie says, forget about
All that. He *is* the best within
And without. She should know. She has
Anger management problems too. Tell the truth,
Same with Billy, same with us all.

Treats from Armando

Maisie was all over Armando,
Hadn't seen him for a week:
Close friends, millions of years:
What a chance meeting him
Where he sits in the woods!
Much embracing, much scratching
Where she likes to be scratched.
And then he said, how about
A treat? And from his little box
He took out a treat.
Maisie looked at it
And said yes. She ate
One piece and then another.
And I said, you know
She always cared about you
Way before she ever got
A treat. So it's not the treats,
He said, but she likes the treats too.

Maisie Meets Armando After Sicknesses of Both

When we left town
Armando was sick—
Taking on water:
A bad sign, everyone knows.
Despite her cancer, Maisie was doing terrific—
Running around and, as always, happy
To see him.

Now she's doing poorly—
Just when he's finally come back.
We'll have to see.
But today, when they met,
They were both at the heart of life:
She rolling on her back,
He working her all over.
That lovefest won't run on
Beyond the death of one of them
But it will ride right up
To the door.

We Fail to Meet Armando on a Day When Rain Is Expected, with Simple and Complicated Responses

It's going to rain today.
All signs are bad
And, as I suspect,
When we pass his bench
Armando's not there.
Poor Maisie: she's desolate
But then sees something else
And moves on. I'm not sure
Myself. It's always a great
Pleasure to talk with him.
He has so many good things
To think about—like the deaths
Of raccoons in the park
From a plague of distemper,
About how he gets the best
Clothes from Macy's
At their drop-off point—
Has to go downtown
Where they stop first.
Or would I rather have Maisie
To myself in the woodland
And its quiet comfort?
I don't know. I know which
Maisie would choose if she could.

Armando Offers Comfort

She went under the knife
For mean breast cancers:
Once, twice, three times—
Ragged gashes in her
Lovely white belly, not wide
But ten days each healing.
Not much pain as I
Could tell. Should I
Have had her spayed?
That was my question
To myself. And it bothered
Me and bothered me.
Maybe I could have spared
Her the belly shave,
The cruel cuts,
The stitches one after
Another, that collar
Which she had to wear
So she didn't pull
Them out. I said
Maybe I did wrong.
Why didn't I do
What the others did?
Armando looked in her eyes
One day—big wolf eyes—
And said: there's so much life
In those eyes. And I
Felt a little better.

Armando Still Wants Maisie's Coat

Now Armando has many fond dog friends.
But he still loves Maisie.
And I think how many times he's said,
Are you going to give that rich coat
To me, that nice warm coat, when winter comes?

Armando's Den in the Park Is Discovered (by No Person)

Armando told our friend Billy
He had a face-to-face in the park.
About four in the morning he was sleeping
In the den he had found and nobody
Else knows: no blizzards can blow on him
And the heat of summer disturbs
Not at all. He heard a little patter
And a sniffing sound. He turned on
His little light and looked up from his hole.
He was bound; eyes locked together:
Curiosity, fear, acceptance. It was
The park's own coyote. Armando unhooked
For an instant and the animal moved,
Flicked its ears and left. Armando went back to sleep.
At least, Billy was sure he went back to sleep.

Maisie Visits Armando *in extremis* and We Talk Little

There's nothing good
Or nice
Or hopeful
Or cute
To say about Maisie
These last days
Except that
Thank god
They haven't come yet.

Armando Happens on Maisie Doing Poorly, Maybe Says Goodbye

Maisie grew old, grew sick,
Recovered, sick again.
They gave her three months to live.
Three years later she lost hair,
Lost the use of her back legs.
She went to the park in a warehouse cart—
No baby carriage for her:
So heavy to lift up each time
And anyway too big to fit.
She missed Armando
But too far to drag that cart
Into the park ramble,
Site of his daily dog court.
So far the bumpy cart could not
Go. She missed him. I could see
Her looking over and down his way.
One day he came past us—
On his way to shop.
What a reunion!
What a love festival!
Don't be jealous,
Armando said to me:
She loves me better than you
And I love her better than you do.
And your cart runs better
Than mine, too, I said.
I was so happy they could meet
And maybe say goodbye.

He said, dogs accept the way
It is today, don't regret
Or look back. When he was
Gone, I wasn't sure of that—
The way Maisie looked after him.

Tale's End

The end of this story
Is too sad to detail—
So I'll just block
It out. Maisie recovered
Somewhat, walked unsteady,
But walked. Visited Armando
Once. Came three cold cold days
And she would visit him
Whatever I said. And she
Missed him three days
Running. She grieved then.
The third, the coldest, she
Caught a chill, and pneumonia,
Went home to die indoors
Within three days. Never had
A chance to hug goodbye
To her dear Armando—
Who never forgets her
The few times now we meet:
Says she was fine, and caring—
And what a splendid coat
She carried! The best.

About the Author

John Maynard is Professor of English Emeritus at NYU. He has published five nonfiction books, including three with Harvard and Cambridge, and many articles and has done a great deal of editing, including co-editing a journal for Cambridge for 26 years. He won the Thomas J. Wilson Prize for his biography of Robert Browning. He was awarded a Guggenheim Fellowship and also an NEH Grant; recently he was given an Albert Nelson Marquis Lifetime Achievement Award by Marquis Who's Who. He is a member of PEN.

During most of his adult life, he wrote some poems and planned to write more. As he neared retirement, he found time to write many more poems, often while walking his golden-doodle Maisie in Central Park. He has been editing them for book publications for the past four years. *Armando and Maisie* is the first of a number of books he plans. Another, *What's It Like to Be Old?*, will be published in 2026. Two more are already completed.

www.ingramcontent.com/pod-product-compliance
Lightning Source LLC
Chambersburg PA
CBHW031205160426
43193CB00008B/511